'From blood, sweat, tears and burn
and a gran in pink socks, the pupils of Len
quick of the human condition in words and pictures with help from
two of Scotland's masters of the craft.'

Jan Patience, arts journalist, *The Herald*

'The writers described their subjects with real honesty and
emotional truth.'

Anne Donovan, author of *Buddha Da*

'A rabbit, a deer, a dolphin, a zoo; on the compelling (in every
sense) evidence of these poems and pictures, maybe every bird and
beast is, 'The Independent Animal'. That confident originality extends
to the affectingly mature meditations on Sadness, Jealousy and other
topics too weighty for the average poem or print. But then these
renderings are far from average as the depictions of brothers and
sisters and other family members demonstrate. A cracking anthology
that will entice and enthrall.'

Donny O'Rourke, poet, journalist, broadcaster

'If poetry is language in orbit, as Seamus Heaney says, then
Cutting Verse represents "lift-off", and these young people are aiming
high - only to be expected when Liz Lochhead and Willie Rodger are
lighting the fuses.'

Peter McCormack, curator, Auld Kirk Museum

'The poems are breathtaking – 'blood coloured teeth' and the
'Smell of Water dripping from the sky' - and the images assured. A
tribute to Willie Rodger and Liz Lochead's inspiration.'

Jane Cameron, curator, University of Stirling

Cutting Verse

Cutting Verse

Lenzie Academy

A Media Matters Book

First published in 2010 by
Media Matters Education Consultancy Ltd
104 Barscube Terrace
Paisley
PA2 6XH
www.mediamatters.co.uk

ISBN 978-1-907693-00-7

The rights of the individual writers of the poems comprising this anthology and the rights of the individual artists as illustrators have been asserted by them in accordance with the Copyright, Designs and Patents Act 1988.

Front Cover: © Kiera Nicol
Back Cover: © Jennifer Miller

Printed in the Great Britain by Lightning Source UK Ltd

Published by Media Matters Education Consultancy Ltd
in association with East Dunbartonshire Council.

sustainable thriving achieving
East Dunbartonshire Council
www.eastdunbarton.gov.uk

For Karen Kerr

The creation, marketing and selling of this book is being run as a
social enterprise with net profits being donated to the
Teenage Cancer Trust.

PREFACE

I am delighted to be asked to provide a preface to *Cutting Verse*, this excellent anthology of poems and prints developed by our young people at Lenzie Academy.

This book is the culmination of the *Joined Up Learning* initiative, which has involved three groups of pupils performing varied tasks, with the support of professionals from the literary, artistic and commercial worlds.

S1 English pupils provided the poems, with advice from the renowned poet Liz Lochhead, while S3 Art and Design pupils provided the illustrations assisted by the artist Willie Rodger, and S3 Business Management students have worked with Birlinn Publishers and the Milngavie Bookshop in producing, marketing and selling this book.

These young people have gained a valuable insight into the professional world of poetry, art and publishing.

I am sure that you will find the poems thought-provoking and inspiring and be equally impressed by the excellent illustrations.

In conclusion, I would wish to thank all involved for their superb contributions to this project.

RJ McLelland
Headteacher
May 2010

CONTENTS

PART I

PART II

PART III

APPENDICES

LINO-CUTS

LINO-CUTS

Willie Rodger, RSA

FOREWORD

BY LIZ LOCHHEAD

When working with East Dunbartonshire secondary schools last Autumn on my part of this creative writing and making-of-a-book initiative -- via GLOW, the ground-breaking, Scotland-wide, first national intranet for Education, no less! -- I kept thinking of my friend Adrian Mitchell, the poet, who died just over a year ago. Adrian would have loved this book. He loved going in to schools and sharing his poems with pupils, and he loved encouraging and helping pupils to write their own -- and he used to put at the start of all his books that none of the poems in it were to be used for any Examination Purposes whatsoever!

Here is an extract from something he wrote about the point of poetry, and of poets:

It is the job of poets to arouse all those parts of the imagination which are asleep or numb. To feed the imagination, to extend the imagination. To use the imagination, to defend the imagination. To explore the imagination. To risk drowning in the imagination.

To be fools. To be glad when they are called fools. To be reminders of doom when they are asked for jokes. To be relentless comedians when asked to be serious.

To be jugglers of images, verbal clowns......

To overcome their own fears. To show people how fears can be overcome, slowly, one by one.

To celebrate life. To attack the enemies of life...

Foreword: Liz Lochhead

Waking up our own imaginations is important work. Easy when we realise that our five sound senses (if we are lucky enough to have all five of them) and the real world around us, and our memory, and the simple truth (which is rarely simple) and the plain ordinary words we use every day (better, far better, than any of those swallowed-a-dictionary ones) are all we need.

And a pencil or a biro and a jotter.

Oh, the marvels of computers, and webcams – and GLOW, when it was up and working... Now, I'm far less technology-literate than most of the pupils I met, but I can say it was truly amazing to go into nine classes simultaneously and for us to do a 'creative writing workshop' in real time together. Later on, it was even better to go (webcam again) into one class at a time and talk face-to-face with pupils about the work they had posted each week. It was great, from the computer on my desktop at home, to go into the pages and read the drafts and rewrites as they got posted – and, best of all, explore the feedback (mostly praise, but lots of friendly and very constructive criticism too!) that these young poets were getting, not only from their own classmates, but also, more and more as we got further into it, from pupils -- and teachers -- in other schools. Colleagues they had only met in this virtual environment. Communication though! Real communication.

From the moment you open Lenzie Academy's *Cutting Verse*, enjoying the word play that celebrates the lino-cutting process as well as the sharpness it suggests in the poetry to come, you'll be first of all in a world of creatures. An empathetically drawn zoo prisoner; the dog Arnie who *'nearly knocks me off my feet/ then licks my face with his sandpaper tongue'*; a coolly, clearly described very dead deer hanging as venison meat outside the butcher's freezer. And more.

14

Then you'll quickly find yourself in a whole section on emotions, starkly titled, which, of course mean nothing at all without concrete images, smells, tastes, sounds, colours and physical sensations to make them live.

Lastly you'll meet family and others. I think that'll be for family and friends of the authors the most moving bit of the book. It is for me. All of these very specific individuals are celebrated by accurate, always perceptively observed details, the wee quirks that make the subject come off the page as that unique human being. You'll experience this book like this *if* you read it from beginning to end rather than dipping in and out of its treasures at random, as this lucky-bag of an anthology invites you to do...

The teachers worked incredibly hard on this. The pupils too, who were often spoilt for choice about what piece or pieces to put into the book, they had achieved so much - usually three poems which had gone through several drafts. I hope they are all as proud and pleased to be in print here as they ought to be.

My friend Willie Rodger, the great printmaker and artist, once again via GLOW, did workshops on both lino-cutting and illustration – how important to get to the essence of something, how vital to be simple, do just one idea, strong and clear. The poets, as they handed over their work to their partner in the Art Class, would, I know, have recognised this paring-down. Exactly the same go-for-it, cut-to-the-chase process they had just gone through.

This book, I'm sure you'll agree, would be so much less without its illustrations. They are strong, subtle, funny, bold, beautiful in turn. The medium of the lino-print, the black ink on the white page, grants a unity to an astonishing range of styles and images. All independent of, but complementing, the words that inspired them.

Foreword: Liz Lochhead

As I write this foreword, feeling excited as I look, online once again, at the projected design and lay-out of this very volume which you now hold in your hand, I realise I have already learned a lot, second-hand, from this enterprise the Business Education pupils are now embarked upon, about the production of, and distribution of, books. (And I thought I was a professional as well!)

The decisions made – after all the passionate arguments -- about the best choice of title, which charity ought to benefit, the design of the cover, how to price it, the publicity for and the marketing of it, have all required a lot more of that communication between different authors, artists, individuals, classes and disciplines in the school. More of that wonderful thing the whole world needs more of: Joined-Up Learning.

Liz Lochhead March 2010

PART I

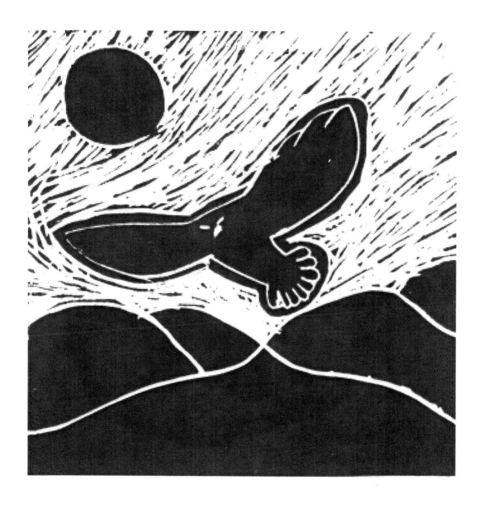

Kierra Nicol

Arnie

I can hear his jagged paws scratching on the wooden floor.
As I call his name,
He comes pounding towards me and nearly knocks me off my feet.
Then he licks my face with his sandpaper tongue
Until I laugh and push him away.

I can see
His four pointy legs and curvy tail,
His two black button eyes,
His wrinkly lumpy skin,
His bronze coloured coat.
It wraps around me like a soft duvet that keeps me warm.

Courtney Lynch

Rabbit Remembrance

You are shaking with fear
because you are worried about your rabbit in the back garden
while that vicious fox is lurking around the estate.
It is December 16th and the ground outside is crisp with light snow.
You are distracted by the snowflakes falling gently outside.

The school bell rings and you are flushed with relief.
You hurry to the bus stop to get the bus home.
The only thought that is in your head is your rabbit.
You see the bus coming and quickly pull yourself onto it
show the driver your bus pass
and sit down next to a bunch of girls wearing lots of make up
and gossiping.
It's your stop.
You stand up, your face flushed with cold sweat.
You are still anxious about your rabbit.

You open the garden gate and scurry round to the back garden
to find the fox
running off into the distance.
You quickly check inside the rabbit's hutch to see if it's alright.
You are horrified...

Ariana Kazeminia

Dolphins

That day I went on holiday.
The day was hot; the night was cold.
Everything changed when the dolphins came -
The smell of ratty salty fish in the water,
The look of the water dancing, as the dolphins jump happily.

I remember the night where the dolphins
squeaked happily in the water,
The sound of crying as the dolphins swam away,
Sand blowing in their faces,
Seagulls stealing the fish from the dolphins' mouths,
The intelligence of a lovely mammal.

The day I said goodbye
Was one of the worst days of my life -
That squeaky noise of remembrance,
The twinkle in the dolphin's eyes,
The loving feeling at home.

Olivia Guild

The Independent Animal

As graceful as a ballet dancer,
Lonely so lonely.
Hunted as if it was a game but
No one is playing.

Its eyes are like diamonds on a bit of coal,
Shining to the world.
It glides down the sky like a hang-glider.
It sees the clear blue sky every day in its life.
It is proud like a father seeing his baby walk.

Mason Miller

Jennifer Miller

24

The Zoo

My eyes were transfixed by its cold stare.
I could see its slicing, cutting claws.
I could feel the cold harsh bars
Separating us from the killing machine inside.
I could see its powerful muscles.
I could smell the rotting meat of its last meal.
My eyes could not look away from its huge
Crushing, biting, ripping teeth.
I could smell the stench
Coming from the creatures huge mouth.
I could hear the deafening roar of the huge beast.
I could hear small bones being crushed
Under its powerful paws.

Glen Glover

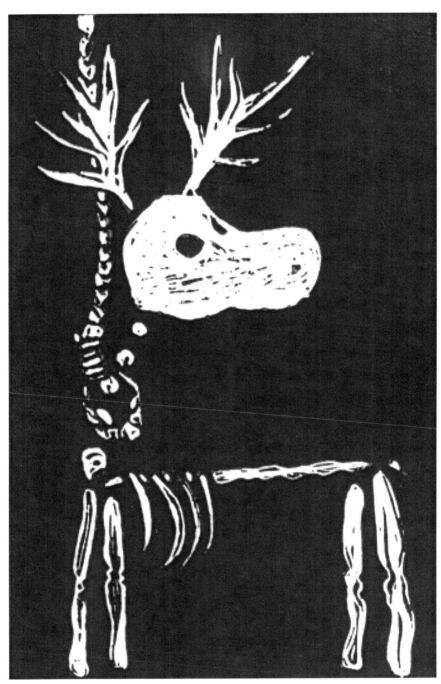

Emma Trussler

The Deer

Walking into the giant freezer,
Seeing the head hanging,
Spinning slowly on a white rope,
With blood coloured teeth.

The freezer was cold, massive, blank and odorous.

The eyes were motionless, bloodshot and staring.

The head was swinging, proud and simply dead.

Jack Bunyan

PART II

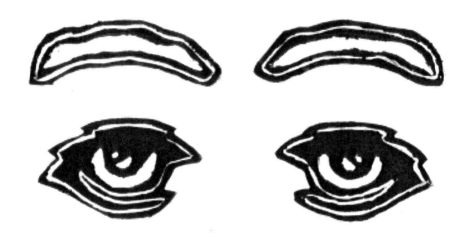

Katie McCulloch-Roberts

Sadness

Sound of pain and crying
Feeling of death and hurt
Smell of water dripping from the sky,
A deep blue colour dripping onto the ground
When I speak I cry my eyes out,
Splashing in every puddle I see,
A feeling of love and heart beating fast

From yellow summer colours, to dark soggy wet colours,
Bright sky fading away while the rain and storm come
The joy from playing to the tears from falling,
The fun and happiness to the blood and sadness
When I close my eyes, I feel safe,
When I open them my mother is there to comfort me

All I want to do is run away,
Let the pain out by crying for hours,
Someone to be there for me,
Through thick and thin,
That is what sadness is all about

Olivia Guild

Guilt

I have stolen £10 from my friend's purse because we had a fight and all I wanted was revenge.

When my friend found out the money was missing, she had a fit and asked me to help her find it.

I did.

Just to look innocent, of course…

GUILT: You are looking at yourself in the mirror.

Only seeing the negative points.

You are furious but at the same time want to clear your guilty conscience.

What will you do?

You feel like the world is against you.

You are holding the note in your hand.

It alters from a brown to a grey black and dark blue.

The pewter colour stares at you.

You feel your stomach churning.

It is going round and round like a washing machine on full speed.

You feel thick liquid rise in your throat.

You go to put the note down

but you catch a glimpse of a message written on the back of the note.

It reads, "These are the colours of guilt.

You are experiencing what real guilt feels like."

You quickly put the note in the drawer nearest to you
and slam it shut.
You suddenly hear a resounding scream.
You make out it's saying, "Feel guilty and apologise!"
You hardly had any sleep last night.
You are positive you have to give the note back now.

Ariana Kazeminia

Laura Barker

Jealousy

Jealousy is a warm cup of coffee,
Seeing a new toy in the shop window,
An old man watching energetic kids run by,
When you see your friend goes away on a tropical holiday.
Jealousy is watching the trailer for a movie.

It is seeing your best friend get a new pet,
When the summer holidays are only days away.
Jealousy could be heaven when you are not there.
It is seeing red roses in a newly cut field,
And smelling the smell from a chip shop.

Jealousy is when your life is coming to a close
and you see a young couple
with their new born baby.

Robbie Fraser

Amy Martin

35

Time

Time is like a great river never stopping and never faltering.

Alasdair Moireasdan

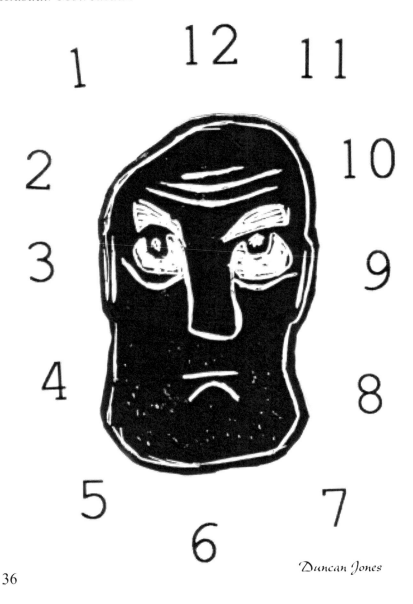

Duncan Jones

Theft

I wear a dark cloak and black sunglasses,
As I wander the streets at night
Looking for things that are valuable and precious.

I sit at my desk and plan the crime,
With my cold hand holding the pencil with a tight grasp.
I am scared, yet excited.

The day has come for me.
As I make the final preparations,
I have a feeling that this is all going to go well.

I can already hear the jewellers screaming,
As I hit the glass with the sledge hammer.
And hear the sirens as I run into the darkness.

Jack Bunyan

Understanding

I am an old man with grey hair wearing a lab coat.
I'm eating porridge as I mix feelings in my lab.
After my porridge, I tick tock like a clock
as I feast on my shiny apple.

Lewis Byron

Hurt

Hurt is a grieving mother visiting her son's grave.
Hurt is loneliness.
Hurt is homelessness.
Hurt is death.
Hurt is war.
Hurt is divorce.
Hurt is pain.
Hurt is crying.
Hurt is abuse.
Hurt is defeat.

Glen Glover

Slavery

They moan and groan: they ache and cry.
The whip lashes: scars appear.
They feel the rough stones under their bare feet.
The smell of sweat is in the air.
They cling onto hope and freedom,
as their masters eat away their souls.
He laughs; they cry.
He smiles; they copy, but upside down.
Eighteen hours a day, under the southern sun.

Ross McLean

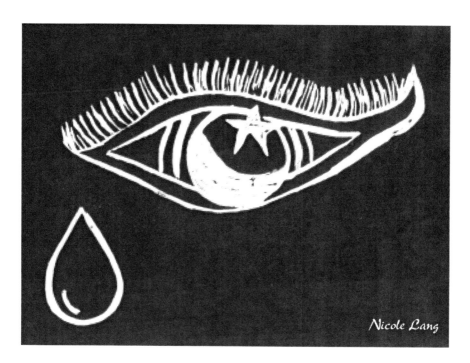

Nicole Lang

Ciaran Summers

RAGE!

Rage smells like gas, powerful and deadly.

Rage feels like glass, sharp and harmful.

Rage looks like the devil, horrible and evil.

Rage sounds like screaming, loud and terrifying.

Rage tastes like burnt toast, warm and disgusting.

Rage is watching you laughing and planning.

Rage, you are nasty, upsetting and scary.

Rage has no laughter, no forgiveness, no happiness.

Rage, we are like death, silent and unstoppable.

Chloe Reid

War

I am screaming.
I am covered in blood.
I am the darkest shade of red.
I wear bullet-proof armour.
I taste of black smoke.
I smell of thick gas.
I am thousands of explosions.
I smell of sweat.
My eyes are dead.
My arms carry a gun.
I cannot be reasoned with.
I fight till the death.
I destroy countries.

Ross McFarlane

Rachel Lang

PART III

Iona Lamont

46

Sister

She is a small noisy child
That is very wild. She always
Has something to say and if she
Doesn't get her way she will make
Everyone pay. She doesn't like when
People give her into trouble because she will
Begin to cry. She will cry until she is livid
And then when someone says they are sorry,
She will start to come round.

In the middle of the night you'll wake up
And get a fright because she's talking in her
Sleep and then you will get to sleep and you are off
In loo loo land and then she will wake you up and
Say "Time for school", and then you can't wait until
She goes to school.

Sean Casey

Lucy

Lucy smiles shyly and hides behind her Granny.
She laughs as we attempt to be funny.
Her thin lips attack her tiny face with a massive gleaming smile.
Her bedtime blanket wraps itself softly round her body.

"Up?" she says in a hopeful voice.
She stretches both arms up above her head
And smiles ever so beautifully, as her feet come off the ground
And she feels warm arms round her to guarantee she won't fall down.

We try to remember jokes that made us laugh
When we were only three years of age.
One slips into memory
We can tell she doesn't understand.

But Lucy laughs
Then drifts away
Into a quiet
Peaceful sleep.

Heather Davis

Kirstyn Wallace

My Big Sister

My big sister is always looking her best.
She is always putting on make-up and smelling of perfume.

My big sister likes to scream, especially at me.
If I say something she doesn't like, she will scream at me all day.

Emma Lochhead

Ewen Cameron

My Big Sister

My big sister likes to wear makeup,
To look good.
Her small hands smudging her foundation all over her face
In a slow, accurate way.
She doesn't like talking while rubbing it in
But shakes nervously trying to get it right.

My sister doesn't enjoy the morning,
Having to get ready for school,
straighteners turned on and
Boiling hot.
"They will burn your skin," I say.

Mason Miller

Big Brother

I like to watch my big brother play football,
His lightning fast speed,
His brilliant passes.
His brain thinks twenty times faster on a football pitch,
The smell of boots after a match,
The mud-coloured socks and
The sweat-covered jersey.

My big brother bullies me constantly.
He punches and kicks me.
He thinks it is funny,
He says that it is my fault.
I don't even do a thing.

Ross McFarlane

Leanne Brown

My Brother

When I see my brother play football
I see him skip by players with ease.
While he is playing,
I smell the steam coming from fresh hotdogs,
newly cut grass.
I hear the chants and celebrations as it is a wonderful game
(best of the season).
I feel that victory is in sight for my brother's team
while the wind is strengthening and becoming more rapid.
I taste the envy between both sides of the football match
which is what everyone wants to taste.
What a game!

Dylan Ryan

My Brother

My brother always plays his electric guitar.
He plays in the day: he plays in the night.
He plays just about all the time.
He always turns the amp up full volume,
So each pluck of a string makes a loud BOOM!

Sometimes, I like to listen to him,
But most of the time, he deafens me.
He takes out all of his anger on his guitar.

He wobbles the whammy bar like he's trying to snap it off.
The whole house shakes like the foundations have gone soft.

Lewis Byron

57

Poem for My Brother

He plays guitar, a nice tune.
He taps me till I answer him.
It's annoying.
He sings whilst playing, Plain White Tee's, *"Hey there Delilah"*.
He LOVES cheeseburgers,
greasy, ketchup-covered cheeseburgers.
He scoffs one up in 10 bites, 20 seconds, a new record.
Sometimes he is alright: other times I can't stand him.

Kevin Riach

My Dad at Work

My dad seems to always be at work.

Even at home he's always on the phone to 'Kenny' and the like.

He seems to always be "on call", darting around

from the "Hill" to the Royal and back.

He'll return at ten at night, all muddy on his bike.

If he's not cycling, he'll drive,

In his battered old Audi, suit and tie,

Listening to 96.5.

Ross McLean

Abbie Wood

My Dad

My Dad loves his guitars.
We have six of them in the house.
He plinks and plunks the same old tune,
We're lucky if we hear something new!

While he sits upon his chair,
Guitar in one hand, remote control in the other.
A huge grin spreads across his face
As his feet move so quickly with his floppy slippers on
They usually never stop!

My Dad loves cycling races on the TV,
He shouts "YES!YES!WE WON!"
That's what makes his feet move so quickly.

It all looks so strange to me…

Holly Michie

My Mother

My mum is the most committed,
Caring and hard-working person I know.
She has a difficult job and works eight until five,
And still comes home and does the washing up and makes the
delicious dinner when she comes home.

Even though I'm twelve,
She still comes in and whispers in her bright Scottish accent
"Goodnight"
In her favourite long brown dressing-gown,
And tries to tuck me in.
Strangely though, I still play along, because I know she misses
when I was a playful child.

Euan MacKintosh

Charlotte Dougall

My Mum

When we walk out of Asda with bundles of shopping
I can see in her face there is something wrong.
It looks puzzled and confused.
Then she looks down at me and says,
"Where did we park the car?'
I look back at her in confusion
But say nothing.

When she is on the phone to her friends
She talks as loud as she can.
It is like listening to a foghorn
Except louder.
She also likes to laugh so loud
It is like a witch cackling
Over a pot of spells.

Courtney Lynch

My Gran

My Gran sits on the couch,
Drinking her Irn Bru,
Watching Hallmark and stroking her cat.
When she stands up, I tower over her.
She is about 4 ft 10.

I like to watch my Gran in the kitchen,
Making Christmas dinner,
Cooking the turkey and beef.

I like to watch my Gran come in from work.
She has her hat and her jacket on
with her pink fluffy socks so her feet don't get cold.

Chloe Reid

ACKNOWLEDGEMENTS

There are a number of people without whose diligence, encouragement and generosity this initiative would not have been possible.

I would like to thank Liz Lochhead for the way in which she gave of her time, and her willingness to share her expertise with the pupils. Monitoring the progress being made by 185 pupils within the English classes as they developed their poems was a major undertaking but one which she undertook with enthusiasm and energy. The pupils have benefitted greatly.

Special thanks also goes to Willie Rodger, who followed on, working with 150 pupils in the Art & Design classes as they sought to illustrate the poems written in English. He gave of his time generously and took a genuine interest in the work of each and every pupil.

As the poetry books have been produced, Vikki Reilly, of Birlinn Books and Susan Frize, of Milngavie Bookshop must also be thanked for their advice and support of the Business Education classes and Enterprise groups.

My personal thanks goes to the Lenzie Academy teachers for their enthusiasm. They have led their pupils through every stage of the learning process with a professionalism which has been greatly appreciated, to Iain McKinstry, of the English department, to Ailsa Mitchell, of the Art & Design Department, to Gillian Scott, of the Business Education Department and to Morag Elliott, Depute Head who has co-ordinated the involvement of each department.

Thanks is also due to East Dunbartonshire Council which made it possible for both staff and pupils to work with the professionals and for the pupils to become published writers and artists themselves.

Above all, I would like to thank the young writers, artists and entrepreneurs who have taken this initiative to their hearts and made this book and its success a reality.

Angela McEwan
Editor

Liz Lochhead was born in Lanarkshire and was educated at Dalziel High School, Motherwell. Later she studied at Glasgow School of Art and graduated with a D.A. from the department of Drawing and Painting. She worked as an Art & Design teacher in various schools in the west of Scotland and England.

Her first collection of poetry was published in 1972. Several collections have been published since that time, the last one being *The Colour of Black and White*. During the 1980s she began writing plays which have been performed by the major Scottish theatre companies. Many of these, including *Mary Queen of Scots Got Her Head Chopped Off,* are in print.

Since 2005, Liz Lochhead has been Glasgow's Poet Laureate. She has been honoured by ten Scottish universities and various arts institutions.

Willie Rodger was born in Kirkintilloch and was educated at Lenzie Academy. He studied at Glasgow School of Art and graduated with a D.A. (Commercial and Graphic Design). Following a year as a graphic visualiser in advertising, he trained as an Art & Design teacher and taught in both Lenzie Academy and then as principal teacher in Clydebank High School.

Since 1954, work has been exhibited at both one-man and group exhibitions at major venues including the Open Eye, the Royal Scottish Academy, the Society of Scottish Arts. His work is exhibited at the Victoria & Albert Museum. He has also undertaken a range of design commissions. He collaborated with Liz Lochhead on her book, *The Colour of Black and White*, providing the lino-print illustrations for the book.

Willie Rodger is a fellow of the Royal Scottish Academy and in 1999 was made an honorary doctor of the University of Stirling.

Joined Up Learning

As nine English classes in nine secondary schools worked together with poet, Liz Lochhead, the talk was about whether this word or that word was exactly right for the impression intended, whether this line length or that line length was the most effective. The pupils worked for six weeks (October - December 2009) developing their poems, changing them, explaining them and commenting on the 'work in progress' in each other's online 'jotter'. The internet was used to link the nine classes to each other and to Liz Lochhead, in discussion forums, in chat rooms and meeting together in live video conferences for tutorials on their work.

Liz, too, tried some of the writing tasks she set and commented - on their work and on her own. Some of the writers were in first year, some were in sixth year but they worked together to improve the writing, theirs and everyone else's... writing, reading, talking, listening, connected through a virtual classroom which included every secondary school in East Dunbartonshire and 185 pupils.

Six weeks on, each of the nine English classes met with an Art & Design class in their own school, and all eighteen classes linked together live online with both Liz Lochhead and Scotland's leading printmaker, Willie Rodger as Liz and Willie explained how he had illustrated her poetry collection, *The Colour of Black & White*. Each Art & Design class then worked with Willie Rodger between January and March 2010, developing, refining and refining their ideas for the prints which would illustrate each of the poems assigned to them by the English classes. The 150 art and design pupils learnt, first hand, the importance of their sketchbooks and how to cut images in lino.

Six weeks on, illustrated anthologies, featuring the poems and prints from each school, went into production. Business Education classes in seven of the schools and Enterprise groups in the other two met Vikki Reilly from publisher, Birlinn Books and Susan Frize, from independent bookseller, The Milngavie Bookshop in an online link to learn about and discuss together the marketing and selling of books.

Those 158 pupils involved in this third stage have the responsibility of selling the illustrated poetry anthologies - of which this book is one - to their own customers, as well as to independent bookshops and major booksellers. They are running book events in their schools and creating an online presence.

As with the English classes and the Art & Design classes, Business Education classes and Enterprise groups are linked together online, sharing ideas and acting as nine Social Enterprises, with net profits from the sale of each book going to a range of charities chosen by the pupils taking part in each school.

Lenzie Academy has chosen to support the Teenage Cancer Trust.

'Joined Up Learning' is a unique initiative in which pupils from different year groups and from different departments within each school have not only worked together but also with English or Art & Design or Business Education classes and Enterprise groups from every other secondary school in their local authority.

Staff in each school have worked together with their subject colleagues in the other schools and with teachers from other departments in their own school, using internet technology to enhance teaching and learning.

*English, Art & Design, Business Education,
Enterprise, Literacy, Numeracy, Citizenship, ICT*

Curriculum for Excellence in Action

Joined Up Learning Series

'The relationship between writing and drawing is immediate and ancient, visible at first glance to the page, but also rising from a long tradition of complementary work between poets and writers and artists of all kinds: the connection is clear if you think about what words like image, line, form and rhythm really mean. All the work in this series of books is galvanized by this connection. Each singular example is a kind of revelation of unsuspected insight, an illumination. And at its best, when this kind of illumination gives you something you really could not have predicted before, you take with you something worth keeping in mind. The creative potential of young people is our richest resource for the future. These books show what good provision can bring. Beyond the storms and droughts, there is evidence here of good weather ahead.'

Professor Alan Riach, Chair of Scottish literature, Glasgow University

'I very much enjoyed reading these collections. I was struck by the emotional honesty of the writers, as well as the beautifully crafted language and the energy and joy they conveyed. The wonderful illustrations worked beautifully with the text, making these books a real delight.'

Anne Donovan, author of *Buddha Da*

'What wonderful collections! Each one engages head, heart and eye. The black and white illustrations capture subject and mood in strikingly original forms.'

Christine Findlay, author of *The Colonel's Collection*

71

'These books represent a fertile collaboration between pupils, teachers, and two very special mentors in the disciplines of art and literature: an alliance through which ideas and inspiration have passed as effortlessly as light through glass.

And if the purpose of education is to draw out rather than to put in, then this glorious association has achieved its aim. With inspiration from the poet and playwright, Liz Lochhead and the visual artist Willie Rodger, creative juices have been set flowing. The happy coalition of two separate art forms has amplified the original stimulus, increased its poignancy, and, with no disjunction between style and substance, released the expressive potential that often lies hidden within the ordinary and the everyday.

Moods and feelings have been given a palpable form that transcends visual or emotional origins creating words and images that are acceptable metaphors for life. The lesson has been learned: art confirms the narratives that make sense of our lives. In reflecting their own thoughts and feelings each of these young artists and writers has wheedled from the coarse material of life some fundamental truths about human existence. And by giving permanence to transitory experience they have exposed both a dramatic intensity and a tender beauty in the sincerity of their intentions.'

Anne Ellis, art historian, broadcaster,
and former curator of The Hill House

"Learning is being able to see the relationship between things."
Jean Renoir

THE JOINED UP LEARNING SERIES

From the Den of the Bear   ... Bearsden Academy

Animals, Abstracts & Allsorts
   ... Bishopbriggs Academy

Write Out of Our Heads   ... Boclair Academy

Colour in Shadows   ... Douglas Academy

A Picture Speaks a Thousand Words
   ... Kirkintilloch High School

Cutting Verse   ... Lenzie Academy

Time Flies...   ... Merkland School

Fruitful Thoughts of Adolescents
   ... St Ninian's High School

Picture Perfect Poems   ... Turnbull High School

http://www.mediamatters.co.uk/JoinedUpLearning/

Lightning Source UK Ltd.
Milton Keynes UK
21 May 2010

154482UK00002B/8/P